AF307770

Defoe
Abbott
Marx
Hardy
Montaigne
Machiavelli
Haggard
Chesterton
Cooper
Emerson
Joyce
Austen
Hugo
Eliot
Grimm
Melville
Carroll
Christie
Stoker
Wilde
Maupassant
Byron
Molière
Schiller
Garnett
Goethe
Einstein
Fitzgerald
Engels
Hawthorne
Smith
Kafka
Hall
Cotton
Kipling
Doyle
Dostoyevsky
Willis
Baum
Henry
Nietzsche
Leslie
Dumas
Flaubert
Turgenev
Balzac
Stockton
Vatsyayana
Crane
Burroughs
Verne
Curtis
Tocqueville
Gogol
Vinci
Homer
Widger
Tolstoy
Whitman
Busch
Darwin
Thoreau
Twain
Scott
Plato
Potter
Freud
Zola
Lawrence
Harte
Kant
Jowett
Stevenson
Dickens
Hesse
Burton
London
Descartes
Poe
Aristotle
Wells
Voltaire
Cervantes
Cooke
Hale
James
Hastings
Bunner
Shakespeare
Irving
Richter
Chambers
da
Shaw
Doré
Dante
Swift
Chekhov
Wodehouse
Benedict
Alcott
Pushkin
Newton

 tredition®

tredition was established in 2006 by Sandra Latusseck and Soenke Schulz. Based in Hamburg, Germany, tredition offers publishing solutions to authors and publishing houses, combined with world-wide distribution of printed and digital book content. tredition is uniquely positioned to enable authors and publishing houses to create books on their own terms and without conventional manu-facturing risks.

For more information please visit: www.tredition.com

TREDITION CLASSICS

This book is part of the TREDITION CLASSICS series. The creators of this series are united by passion for literature and driven by the intention of making all public domain books available in printed format again - worldwide. Most TREDITION CLASSICS titles have been out of print and off the bookstore shelves for decades. At tredi-tion we believe that a great book never goes out of style and that its value is eternal. Several mostly non-profit literature projects pro-vide content to tredition. To support their good work, tredition donates a portion of the proceeds from each sold copy. As a reader of a TREDITION CLASSICS book, you support our mission to save many of the amazing works of world literature from oblivion. See all available books at www.tredition.com.

Project Gutenberg

The content for this book has been graciously provided by Project Gutenberg. Project Gutenberg is a non-profit organization founded by Michael Hart in 1971 at the University of Illinois. The mission of Project Gutenberg is simple: To encourage the creation and distribu-tion of eBooks. Project Gutenberg is the first and largest collection of public domain eBooks.

Laperouse

Ernest Scott

Imprint

This book is part of TREDITION CLASSICS

Author: Ernest Scott
Cover design: Buchgut, Berlin – Germany

Publisher: tredition GmbH, Hamburg - Germany
ISBN: 978-3-8424-5491-0

www.tredition.com
www.tredition.de

Laperouse

by

Ernest Scott

DEDICATION
To my friend T.B.E.

CONTENTS

FOREWORD

All Sydney people, and most of those who have visited the city, have seen the tall monument to Laperouse overlooking Botany Bay. Many have perhaps read a little about him, and know the story of his surprising appearance in this harbour six days after the arrival of Governor Phillip with the First Fleet. One can hardy look at the obelisk, and at the tomb of Pere Receveur near by, without picturing the departure of the French ships after bidding farewell to the English officers and colonists. Sitting at the edge of the cliff, one can follow Laperouse out to sea, with the eye of imagination, until sails, poops and hulls diminish to the view and disappear below the hazy-blue horizon. We may be sure that some of Governor Phillip's people watched the sailing, and the lessening, and the melting away of the vessels, from just about the same place, one hundred and twenty four years ago. What they saw, and what we can imagine, was really the end of a romantic career, and the beginning of a mystery of the sea which even yet has not lost its fascination.

The story of that life is surely worth telling, and, we trust, worth reading; for it is that of a good, brave and high-minded man, a great sailor, and a true gentleman. The author has put into these few pages what he has gleaned from many volumes, some of them stout, heavy and dingy tomes, though delightful enough to "those who like that sort of thing." He hopes that the book may for many readers touch with new meaning those old weatherworn stones at Botany Bay, and make the personality of Laperouse live again for such as nourish an interest in Australian history.

ILLUSTRATIONS.

Life of Laperouse

Chapter I.

FAMILY, YOUTH and INFLUENCES

Jean-Francois Galaup, Comte De Laperouse, was born at Albi, on August 23, 1741. His birthplace is the chief town in the Department of Tarn, lying at the centre of the fruitful province of Languedoc, in the south of France. It boasts a fine old Gothic cathedral, enriched with much noble carving and brilliant fresco painting; and its history gives it some importance in the lurid and exciting annals of France. From its name was derived that of a religious sect, the Albigeois, who professed doctrines condemned as heretical and endured severe persecution during the thirteenth century.

But among all the many thousands of men who have been born, and have lived, and died in the old houses of the venerable city, none, not even among its bishops and counts, has borne a name which lives in the memory of mankind as does that of the navigator, Laperouse. The sturdy farmers of the fat and fertile plain which is the granary of France, who drive in to Albi on market days, the patient peasants of the fields, and the simple artisans who ply their primitive trades under the shadow of the dark-red walls of St. Cecile, know few details, perhaps, about the sailor who sank beneath the waters of the Pacific so many years ago. Yet very many of them have heard of Laperouse, and are familiar with his monument cast in bronze in the public square of Albi. They speak his name respectfully as that of one who grew up among their ancestors, who trod their streets, sat in their cathedral, won great fame, and met his death under the strange, distant, southern stars.

His family had for five hundred years been settled, prominent and prosperous, on estates in the valley of the Tarn. In the middle of the fifteenth century a Galaup held distinguished office among the citizens of Albi, and several later ancestors are mentioned honourably in its records. The father of the navigator, Victor Joseph de Galaup, succeeded to property which maintained him in a position of influence and affluence among his neighbours. He married Marguerite de Resseguier, a woman long remembered in the district for her qualities of manner and mind. She exercised a strong influence over her adventurous but affectionate son; and a letter written to her by him at an interesting crisis of his life, testifies to his eager desire to conform to his mother's wishes even in a matter that wrenched his heart, and after years of service in the Navy had taken him far and kept him long from her kind, concerning eyes.

Jean-Francois derived the name by which he is known in history from the estate of Peyrouse, one of the possessions of his family. But he dropped the "y" when assuming the designation, and invariably spelt the name "Laperouse," as one word. Inasmuch as the final authority on the spelling of a personal name is that of the individual who owns it, there can be no doubt that we ought always to spell this name "Laperouse," as, in fact, successors in the family who have borne it have done; though in nearly all books, French as well as English, it is spelt "La Perouse." In the little volume now in the reader's hands, the example of Laperouse himself has been followed.

On this point it may be remarked concerning another navigator who was engaged in Australian exploration, that we may lose touch with an interesting historical fact by not observing the correct form of a name. On maps of Tasmania appears "D'Entrecasteaux Channel." It was named by and after Admiral Bruny Dentrecasteaux, who as commander of the RECHERCHE and ESPERANCE visited Australian waters. We shall have something to say about his expedition towards the close of the book. Now, Dentrecasteaux sailed from France in 1791, while the Revolution was raging. All titles had been abolished by a decree of the National Assembly on July 19th, 1790. When he made this voyage, therefore, the Admiral was not Bruny D'Entrecasteaux, a form which implied a territorial titular distinction; but simply Citizen Dentrecasteaux. The name is so spelt in the contemporary histories of his expedition written by Rossel and Labillardiere. It would not have been likely to be spelt in any other way by a French officer at the time. Thus, the Marquis de la Fayette became simply Lafayette, and so with all other bearers of titles in France. Consequently we should, by observing this little difference, remind ourselves of Dentrecasteaux' period and circumstances.

That, however, is by the way, and our main concern for the present is with Laperouse.

As a boy, Jean-Francois developed a love for books of voyages, and dreamt, as a boy will, of adventures that he would enjoy when he grew to manhood. A relative tells us that his imagination was enkindled by reading of the recent discoveries of Anson. As he grew up, and himself sailed the ocean in command of great ships, he continued to read all the voyaging literature he could procure. The writings of Byron, Carteret, Wallis, Louis de Bougainville, "and above all Cook," are mentioned as those of his heroes. He "burned to follow in their footsteps."

It will be observed that, with one exception, the navigators who are especially described by one of his own family as having influenced the bent of Laperouse were Englishmen. He did not, of course, read all of their works in his boyhood, because some of them were published after he had embraced a naval career. But we note them in this place, as the guiding stars by which he shaped his course. He must have been a young man, already on the way to distinction as an officer, when he came under the spell of Cook. "And above all Cook," says his relative. To the end of his life, down to the final days of his very last voyage, Laperouse revered the name of Cook. Every Australian reader will like him the better for that. Not many months before his own life ended in tragedy and mystery, he visited the island where the great English sailor was slain. When he reflected on the achievements of that wonderful career, he sat down in his cabin and wrote in his Journal the passage of which the following is a translation. It is given here out of its chronological order, but we are dealing with the influences that made Laperouse what he was, and we can see from these sincere and feeling words, what Cook meant to him:

"Full of admiration and of respect as I am for the memory of that great man, he will always be in my eyes the first of navigators. It is he who has determined the precise position of these islands, who has explored their shores, who has made known the manners, customs and religion of the inhabitants, and who has paid with his blood for all the light which we have to-day concerning these peoples. I would call him the Christopher Columbus of these countries, of the coast of Alaska, and of nearly all the isles of the South Seas. Chance might enable the most ignorant man to discover islands, but it belongs only to great men like him to leave nothing more to be done regarding the coasts they have found. Navigators, philosophers, physicians, all find in his Voyages interesting and useful things which were the object of his concern. All men, especially all navigators, owe a tribute of praise to his memory. How could one neglect to pay it at the moment of coming upon the group of islands where he finished so unfortunately his career?"

We can well understand that a lad whose head was full of thoughts of voyaging and adventure, was not, as a schoolboy, very tame and easy to manage. He is described as having been ardent, impetuous, and rather stubborn. But there is more than one kind of stubbornness. There is the stupid stubbornness of the mule, and the fixed, firm will of the intelligent being. We can perceive quite well what is meant in this case. On the other hand, he was affectionate, quick and clever. He longed for the sea; and his father, observing his decided inclination, allowed him to choose the profession he desired.

It may well have seemed to the parents of Laperouse at this time that fine prospects lay before a gallant young gentleman who should enter the Marine. There was for the moment peace between France and England. A truce had been made by the treaty of Aix-la-Chapelle in 1748. But everybody knew that there would be war again soon. Both countries were struggling for the mastery in India and in North America. The sense of rivalry was strong. Jealousies were fierce on both sides. In India, the French power was wielded, and ever more and more extended, by the brilliant Governor Dupleix; whilst in the British possessions the rising influence was that of the dashing, audacious Clive. In North America the French were scheming to push their dominion down the Ohio-Mississippi Valley from Canada to the Gulf of Mexico, in the rear of the line of British colonies planted on the seaboard from the Gulf of St. Lawrence to Florida. The colonists were determined to prevent them; and a young man named George Washington, who afterwards became very famous, first rose into prominence in a series of tough struggles to thwart the French designs. The points of collision between the two nations were so sharp, feeling on either side was so bitter, the contending interests were so incapable of being reconciled, that it was plain to all that another great war was bound to break out, and that sea power would play a very important part in the issue. The young Laperouse wanted to go to sea, and his father wanted him to distinguish himself and confer lustre on his name. The choice of a calling for him, therefore, suited all the parties concerned.

He was a boy of fifteen when, in November, 1756, he entered the Marine service as a royal cadet. He had not long to wait before tasting "delight of battle," for the expected war was declared in May, and before he was much older he was in the thick of it.

Chapter II.

THE FRENCH NAVAL OFFICER.

Laperouse first obtained employment in the French navy in the CELEBRE, from March to November, 1757. From this date until his death, thirty-one years later, he was almost continuously engaged, during peace and war, in the maritime service of his country. The official list of his appointments contains only one blank year, 1764. He had then experienced close upon seven years of continuous sea fighting and had served in as many ships: the CELEBRE, the PO-MONE, the ZEPHIR, the CERF, the FORMIDABLE, the ROBUSTE, and the SIX CORPS. But the peace of Paris was signed in the early part of 1763. After that, having been promoted to the rank of ensign, he had a rest.

It was not a popular peace on either side. In Paris there was a current phrase, "BETE COMME LA PAIX," stupid as the peace. In England, the great Pitt was so indignant on account of its conditions that, all swollen and pinched with gout as he was, he had himself carried to the House of Commons, his limbs blanketted in bandages and his face contorted with pain, and, leaning upon a crutch, denounced it in a speech lasting three hours and forty minutes. The people cheered him to the echo when he came out to his carriage, and the vote favourable to the terms of the treaty was carried by wholesale corruption. But all the same, Great Britain did very well out of it, and both countries—though neither was satisfied—were for the time being tired of war.

For Laperouse the seven years had been full of excitement. The most memorable engagement in which he took part was a very celebrated one, in November, 1759. A stirring ballad has been written about it by Henry Newbolt:—

> "In seventeen hundred and fifty-nine
> When Hawke came swooping from the West,
> The French King's admiral with twenty of the line
> Came sailing forth to sack us out of Brest."

Laperouse's ship, the FORMIDABLE, was one of the French fleet of twenty-one sail. What happened was this. The French foreign minister, Choiseul, had hatched a crafty plan for the invasion of England, but before it could be executed the British fleet had to be cleared out of the way. There was always that tough wooden wall with the hearts of oak behind it, standing solidly in the path. It baffled Napoleon in the same fashion when he thought out an invasion plan in the next century. The French Admiral, Conflans, schemed to lure Sir Edward Hawke into Quiberon Bay, on the coast of Brittany. A strong westerly gale was blowing and was rapidly swelling into a raging tempest. Conflans, piloted by a reliable guide who knew the Bay thoroughly, intended to take up a fairly safe, sheltered position on the lee side, and hoped that the wind would force Hawke, who was not familiar with the ground, on to the reefs and shoals, where his fleet would be destroyed by the storm and the French guns together. But Hawke, whose name signally represents the bold, swift, sure character of the man, understood the design, took the risk, avoided the danger, and clutched the prey. Following the French as rapidly as wind and canvas could take him, he caught their rearmost vessels, smashed them up, battered the whole fleet successively into flight or splinters, and himself lost only two vessels, which ran upon a shoal. Plodding prose does scant justice to the extraordinary brilliancy of Hawke's victory, described by Admiral Mahan as "the Trafalgar of this war." We cannot pass on without quoting one of Mr. Newbolt's graphic verses:—

> "'Twas long past the noon of a wild November day
> When Hawke came swooping from the west;
> He heard the breakers thundering in Quiberon Bay,
> But he flew the flag for battle, line abreast.
> Down upon the quicksands, roaring out of sight,
> Fiercely blew the storm wind, darkly fell the night,
> For they took the foe for pilot and the cannon's glare for
> light,
> When Hawke came swooping from the West."

"They took the foe for pilot:" that is a most excellent touch, both poetical and true.

The FORMIDABLE was the first to be disposed of in the fight. She was an 80-gun line-of-battle ship, carrying the flag of Admiral du Verger. Her position being in the rear of the squadron, she was early engaged by the RESOLUTION, and in addition received the full broadside of every other British ship that passed her. The Admiral fell mortally wounded, and two hundred on board were killed. She struck her colours at four o'clock after receiving a terrible battering, and was the only French ship captured by Hawke's fleet. All the others were sunk, burnt, or beached, or else escaped. The young Laperouse was amongst the wounded, though his hurts were not dangerous; and, after a brief period spent in England as a prisoner of war, he returned to service.

An amusing rhyme in connection with this engagement is worth recalling. Supplies for Hawke's fleet did not come to hand for a considerable time after they were due, and in consequence the victorious crews had to be put on "short commons." Some wag—it is the way of the British sailor to do his grumbling with a spice of humour—put the case thus:—

> "Ere Hawke did bang
> Monsieur Conflans,
> You sent us beef and beer;
> Now Monsieur's beat
> We've nought to eat,
> Since you have nought to fear."

An interesting coincidence must also be noted. Thirty-five years later, only a few leagues from the place where Laperouse first learnt what it meant to fight the British on the sea, another young officer who was afterwards greatly concerned with Australasian exploration had his introduction to naval warfare. It was in 1794 that Midshipman Matthew Flinders, on the BELLEROPHON, Captain Pasley, played his valiant little part in a great fleet action off Brest. Both of these youths, whose longing was for exploration and discovery, and who are remembered by mankind in that connection, were cradled on the sea amidst the smoke and flame of battle, both in the same waters.

During the next twenty-five years Laperouse saw a considerable amount of fighting in the East and West Indies, and in Canadian waters. He was commander of the AMAZON, under D'Estaing, during a period when events did not shape themselves very gloriously for British arms, not because our admirals had lost their skill and nerve, or our seamen their grit and courage, but because Governments at home muddled, squabbled, starved the navy, misunderstood the problem, and generally made a mess of things. We need not follow him through the details of these years, but simply note that Laperouse's dash and good seamanship won him a high reputation among French naval officers, and brought him under the eye of the authorities who afterwards chose him to command an expedition of discovery.

One incident must be recorded, because it throws a light on the character of Laperouse. In 1782, whilst serving under Admiral Latouche-Treville in the West, he was ordered to destroy the British forts on the Hudson River. He attacked them with the SCEPTRE, 74 guns. The British had been engaged in their most unfortunate war with the American Colonies, and in 1781, in consequence of wretchedly bad strategy, had lost command of the sea. The French had been helping the revolted Americans, not for love of them, but from enmity to their rivals. After the capitulation of the British troops at Yorktown, a number of loyalists still held out under discouraging conditions in Canada, and the French desired to dislodge them from the important waterway of the Hudson.

Laperouse found little difficulty in fulfilling his mission, for the defence was weak and the garrisons of the forts, after a brief resistance, fled to the woods. It was then that he did a thing described in our principal naval history as an act of "kindness and humanity, rare in the annals of war." Laperouse knew that if he totally destroyed the stores as well as the forts, the unfortunate British, after he had left, would perish either from hunger or under the tomahawks of the Red Indians. So he was careful to see that the food and clothing, and a quantity of powder and small arms, were left untouched, for, as he nobly said, "An enemy conquered should have nothing more to fear from a civilised foe; he then becomes a friend."

Some readers may like to see the verses in which a French poet has enshrined this incident. For their benefit they are appended:—

"Un jour ayant appris que les Anglais en fuite
Se cachaient dans un bois redoutant la poursuite,
Tu laissas sur la plage aux soldats affames,
Par la peur affoles, en haillons, desarmes,
Des vivres abondantes, des habits et des armes;
Tu t'eloignas apres pour calmer leurs alarmes,
Et quand on s'etonnait: 'Sachez qu' un ennemi
Vaincu n'a rien a craindre, et devient un ami.'"

The passage may be rendered in English thus: "One day, having heard that the fleeing English were hidden in a forest dreading pursuit, you left upon the shore for those soldiers—famished, ragged, disarmed, and paralysed by fear—abundance of food, clothes and arms; then, to calm their fears, you removed your forces to a distance; and, when astonishment was expressed, you said: 'Understand that a beaten enemy has nothing to fear from us, and becomes a friend.'"

Chapter III.

THE LOVE STORY OF LAPEROUSE.

"My story is a romance"—"Mon histoire est un roman"—wrote Laperouse in relating the events with which this chapter will deal. We have seen him as a boy; we have watched him in war; we shall presently follow him as a navigator. But it is just as necessary to read his charming love story, if we are to understand his character. We should have no true idea of him unless we knew how he bore himself amid perplexities that might have led him to quote, as peculiarly appropriate to his own case, the lines of Shakespeare:—

> "Ay me! for ought that ever I could read,
> Could ever hear by tale or history,
> The course of true love never did run smooth,"

During the period of his service in the East Indies, Laperouse frequently visited Ile-de-France (which is now a British possession, called Mauritius). Then it was the principal naval station of the French in the Indian Ocean. There he met a beautiful girl, the daughter of one of the subordinate officials at Port Louis. Louise Eleonore Broudou is said to have been "more than pretty"; she was distinguished by grace of manner, charm of disposition, and fine, cultivated character. The young officer saw her often, admired her much, fell in love with her, and asked her to marry him. Mademoiselle loved him too; and if they two only had had to be consulted, the happy union of a well-matched pair might have followed soon.

It signified little to Laperouse, in love, that the lady had neither rank nor fortune. But his family in France took quite a different view. He wrote to a favourite sister, telling her about it, and she lost no time in conveying the news to his parents. This was in 1775. Then the trouble began.

Inasmuch as he was over thirty years of age at this time, it may be thought that he might have been left to choose a wife for himself. But a young officer of rank in France, under the Old Regime, was not so free in these matters as he would be nowadays. Marriage was much more than a personal affair. It was even more than a family affair. People of rank did not so much marry as "make alliances"—or rather, submit to having them made for them. It was quite a regular thing for a marriage to be arranged by the families of two young people who had never even seen each other. An example of that kind will appear presently.

The idea that the Comte de Laperouse, one of the smartest officers in the French King's navy, should marry out of his rank and station, shocked his relatives and friends as much as it would have done if he had been detected picking pockets. He could not, without grave risk of social and professional ruin, marry until he had obtained the consent of his father, and—so naval regulations required—of his official superiors. Both were firmly refused. Monsieur de Ternay, who commanded on the Ile-de-France station, shook his wise head, and told the lover "that his love fit would pass, and that people did not console themselves for being poor with the fact that they were married." (This M. de Ternay, it may be noted, had commanded a French squadron in Canada in 1762, and James Cook was a junior officer on the British squadron which blockaded him in St. John's Harbour. He managed to slip out one night, much to the disgust of Colville, the British Admiral, who commented scathingly on his "shameful flight.")

The father of Laperouse poured out his forbidding warnings in a long letter. Listen to the "tut-tut" of the old gentleman at Albi:—

"You make me tremble, my son. How can you face with coolness the consequences of a marriage which would bring you into disgrace with the Minister and would lose you the assistance of powerful friends? You would forfeit the sympathies of your colleagues and would sacrifice the fruit of your work during twenty years. In disgracing yourself you would humiliate your family and your parents. You would prepare for yourself nothing but remorse; you would sacrifice your fortune and position to a frivolous fancy for beauty and to pretended charms which perhaps exist only in your own imagination. Neither honour nor probity compels you to meet ill-considered engagements that you may have made with that person or with her parents. Do they or you know that you are not free, that you are under my authority?" He went on to draw a picture of the embarrassments that would follow such a marriage, and then there is a passage revealing the cash-basis aspect of the old gentleman's objection: "You say that there are forty officers in the Marine who have contracted marriages similar to that which you propose to make. You have better models to follow, and in any case what was lacking on the side of birth, in these instances, was compensated by fortune. Without that balance they would not have had the baseness and imprudence to marry thus." Poor Eleonore had no compensating balance of that kind in her favour. She was only beautiful, charming and sweet-natured. Therefore, "tut-tut, my son!"

In the course of the next few months Laperouse covered himself with glory by his services on the AMAZON, the ASTREE, and the SCEPTRE, and he hoped that these exploits would incline his father to accede to his ardent wish. But no; the old gentleman was as hard as a rock. He "tut-tutted" with as much vigour as ever. The lovers had to wait.

Then his mother, full of love for her son and of pride in his achievements, took a hand, and tried to arrange a more suitable match for him. An old friend of the family, Madame de Vesian had a marriageable daughter. She was rich and beautiful, and her lineage was noble. She had never seen Laperouse, and he had never seen her, but that was an insignificant detail in France under the old Regime. If the parents on each side thought the marriage suitable, that was enough. The wishes of the younger people concerned were, it is true, consulted before the betrothal, but it was often a consultation merely in form, and under pressure. We should think that way of making marriages most unsatisfactory; but then, a French family of position in the old days would have thought our freer system very shocking and loose. It is largely a matter of usage; and that the old plan, which seems so faulty to us, produced very many happy and lasting unions, there is much delightful French family history to prove.

Laperouse had now been many months away from Ile-de-France and the bright eyes of Eleonore. He was extremely fond of his mother, and anxious to meet her wishes. Moreover, he held Madame de Vesian in high esteem, and wrote that he "had always admired her, and felt sure that her daughter resembled her." These influences swayed him, and he gave way; but, being frank and honest by disposition, insisted that no secret should be made of his affair of the heart with the lady across the sea. He wrote to Madame de Vesian a candid letter, in which he said:—

"Being extremely sensitive, I should be the most unfortunate of men if I were not beloved by my wife, if I had not her complete confidence, if her life amongst her friends and children did not render her perfectly happy. I desire one day to regard you as a mother, and to-day I open my heart to you as my best friend. I authorise my mother to relate to you my old love affair. My heart has always been a romance (MON COEUR A TOUJOURS ETE UN ROMAN); and the more I sacrificed prudence to those whom I loved the happier I was. But I cannot forget the respect that I owe to my parents and to their wishes. I hope that in a little while I shall be free. If then I have a favourable reply from you, and if I can make your daughter happy and my character is approved, I shall fly to Albi and embrace you a thousand times. I shall not distinguish you from my mother and my sisters."

He also wrote to Monsieur de Vesian, begging him not to interfere with the free inclinations of his daughter, and to remember that "in order to be happy there must be no repugnance to conquer. I have, however," he added, "an affair to terminate which does not permit me to dispose of myself entirely. My mother will tell you the details. I hope to be free in six weeks or two months. My happiness will then be inexpressible if I obtain your consent and that of Madame de Vesian, with the certainty of not having opposed the wishes of Mademoiselle, your daughter."

"I hope to be free"—did he "hope"? That was his polite way of putting the matter. Or he may have believed that he had conquered his love for Eleonore Broudou, and that she, as a French girl who understood his obligations to his family, would—perhaps after making a few handkerchiefs damp with her tears—acquiesce.

So the negotiations went on, and at length, in May, 1783, the de Vesian family accepted Laperouse as the fiance of their daughter. "My project is to live with my family and yours," he wrote. "I hope that my wife will love my mother and my sisters, as I feel that I shall love you and yours. Any other manner of existence is frightful to me, and I have sufficient knowledge of the world and of myself to know that I can only be happy in living thus."

But in the very month that he wrote contracting himself — that is precisely the word — to marry the girl he had never seen, Eleonore, the girl whom he had seen, whom he had loved, and whom he still loved in his heart, came to Paris with her parents. Laperouse saw her again. He told her what had occurred. Of course she wept; what girl would not? She said, between her sobs, that if it was to be all over between them she would go into a convent. She could never marry anyone else.

"Mon histoire est un roman," and here beginneth the new chapter of this real love story. Why, we wonder, has not some novelist discovered these Laperouse letters and founded a tale upon them? Is it not a better story even told in bare outline in these few pages, than nine-tenths of the concoctions of the novelists, which are sold in thousands? Think of the wooing of these two delightful people, the beautiful girl and the gallant sailor, in the ocean isle, with its tropical perfumes and colours, its superb mountain and valley scenery, bathed in eternal sunshine by day and kissed by cool ocean breezes by night — the isle of Paul and Virginia, the isle which to Alexandre Dumas was the Paradise of the World, an enchanted oasis of the ocean, "all carpeted with greenery and refreshed with cooling streams, where, no matter what the season, you may gently sink asleep beneath the shade of palms and jamrosades, soothed by the babbling of a crystal spring."

Think of how he must have entertained and thrilled her with accounts of his adventures: of storms, of fights with the terrible English, of the chasing of corsairs and the battering of the fleets of Indian princes. Think of her open-eyed wonder, and of the awakening of love in her heart; and then of her dread, lest after all, despite his consoling words and soft assurances, he, the Comte, the officer, should be forbidden to marry her, the maiden who had only her youth, her beauty, and her character, but no rank, no fortune, to win favour from the proud people who did not know her. The author is at all events certain of this: that if the letters had seen the light before old Alexandre Dumas died, he would have pounced upon them with glee, and would have written around them a romance that all the world would have rejoiced to read.

But while we think of what the novelists have missed, we are neglecting the real story, the crisis of which we have now reached.

Seeing Eleonore again, his sensitive heart deeply moved by her sorrow, Laperouse took a manly resolution. He would marry her despite all obstacles. He had promised her at her home in Ile-de-France. He would keep his promise. He would not spoil her beautiful young life even for his family.

But there was the contract concerning Mademoiselle de Vesian. What of that? Clearly Laperouse was in a fix. Well, a man who has been over twenty-five years at sea has been in a fix many times, and learns that a bold face and tact are good allies. Remembering the nature of his situation, it will be agreed that the letter he wrote to his mother, announcing his resolve, was a model of good taste and fine feeling:

"I have seen Eleonore, and I have not been able to resist the remorse by which I am devoured. My excessive attachment to you had made me violate all that which is most sacred among men. I forgot the vows of my heart, the cries of my conscience. I was in Paris for twenty days, and, faithful to my promise to you, I did not go to see her. But I received a letter from her. She made no reproach against me, but the most profound sentiment of sadness was expressed in it. At the instant of reading it the veil fell from my eyes. My situation filled me with horror. I am no better in my own eyes than a perjurer, unworthy of Mademoiselle de Vesian, to whom I brought a heart devoured by remorse and by a passion that nothing could extinguish. I was equally unworthy of Mademoiselle Broudou, and wished to leave her. My only excuse, my dear mother, is the extreme desire I have always had to please you. It is for you alone, and for my father, that I wished to marry. Desiring to live with you for the remainder of my life, I consented to your finding me a wife with whom I could abide. The choice of Mademoiselle de Vesian had overwhelmed me, because her mother is a woman for whom I have a true attachment; and Heaven is my witness to-day that I should have preferred her daughter to the most brilliant match in the universe. It is only four days since I wrote to her on the subject. How can I reconcile my letter with my present situation? But, my dear mother, it would be feebleness in me to go further with the engagement. I have doubtless been imprudent in contracting an engagement without your consent, but I should be a monster if I violated my oaths and married Mademoiselle de Vesian. I do not doubt that you tremble at the abyss over which you fear that I am about to fall, but I feel that I can only live with Eleonore, and I hope that you will give your consent to our union. My fortune will suffice for our wants, and we shall live near you. But I shall only come to Albi when Mademoiselle de Vesian shall be married, and when I can be sure that another, a thousand times more worthy than I am, shall have sworn to her an attachment deeper than that which it was in my power to offer. I shall write neither to Madame nor Monsieur de Vesian. Join to your other kindnesses that of undertaking this painful commission."

There was no mistaking the firm, if regretful tone, of that letter; and Laperouse married his Eleonore at Paris.

Did Mademoiselle de Vesian break her heart because her sailor fiance had wed another? Not at all! She at once became engaged to the Baron de Senegas — had she seen him beforehand, one wonders? — and married him in August! Laperouse was prompt to write his congratulations to her parents, and it is diverting to find him saying, concerning the lady to whom he himself had been engaged only a few weeks before, that he regretted "never having had the honour of seeing her!"

But there was still another difficulty to be overcome before Laperouse and his happy young bride could feel secure. He had broken a regulation of the service by marrying without official sanction. True, he had talked of settling down at Albi, but that was when he thought he was going to marry a young lady whom he did not know. Now he had married the girl of his heart; and love, as a rule, does not stifle ambition. Rather are the two mutually co-operative. Eleonore had fallen in love with him as a gallant sailor, and a sailor she wanted him still to be. Perhaps, in her dreams, she saw him a great Admiral, commanding powerful navies and winning glorious victories for France. Madame la Comtesse did not wish her husband to end his career because he had married her, be sure of that.

Here Laperouse did a wise and tactful thing, which showed that he understood something of human nature. Nothing interests old ladies so much as the love affairs of young people; and old ladies in France at that time exercised remarkable influence in affairs of government. The Minister of Marine was the Marquis de Castries. Instead of making a clean breast of matters to him, Laperouse wrote a long and delightful letter to Madame la Marquise. "Madame," he said, "mon histoire est un roman," and he begged her to read it. Of course she did. What old lady would not? She was a very grand lady indeed, was Madame la Marquise; but this officer who wrote his heart's story to her, was a dashing hero. He told her how he had fallen in love in Ile-de-France; how consent to his marriage had been officially and paternally refused; how he had tried "to stifle the sentiments which were nevertheless remaining at the bottom of my heart." Would she intercede with the Minister for him and excuse him?

Of course she would! She was a dear old lady, was Madame la Marquise. Within a few days Laperouse received from the Minister a most paternal, good natured letter, which assured him that his romantic affair should not interfere with his prospects, and concluded: "Enjoy the pleasure of having made someone happy, and the marks of honour and distinction that you have received from your fellow citizens."

Such is the love story of Laperouse. Alas! the marriage did not bring many years of happiness to poor Eleonore, much as she deserved them. Two years afterwards, her hero sailed away on that expedition from which he never returned. She dwelt at Albi, hoping until hope gave way to despair, and at last she died, of sheer grief they said, nine years after the waters of the Pacific had closed over him who had wooed her and wedded her for herself alone.

Chapter IV.

THE VOYAGE OF EXPLORATION.

King Louis XVI of France was as unfortunate a monarch as was ever born to a throne. Had it been his happier lot to be the son of a farmer, a shopkeeper, or a merchant, he would have passed for an excellent man of business and a good, solid, sober, intelligent citizen. But he inherited with his crown a system of government too antiquated for the times, too repressive for the popular temper to endure, and was not statesman enough to remodel it to suit the requirements of his people. It was not his fault that he was not a great man; and a great man—a man of large grasp, wide vision, keen sympathies, and penetrating imagination—was needed in France if the social forces at work, the result of new ideas fermenting in the minds of men and impelling them, were to be directed towards wise and wholesome reform. Failing such direction, those forces burst through the restraints of law, custom, authority, loyalty and respect, and produced the most startling upheaval in modern history, the Great French Revolution. Louis lost both his crown and his head, the whole system of government was overturned, and the way was left open for the masterful mind and strong arm needed to restore discipline and order to the nation: Napoleon Bonaparte.

Louis was very fond of literature. During the sad last months of his imprisonment, before the guillotine took his life, he read over 230 volumes. He especially liked books of travel and geography, and one of his favourite works was the VOYAGES of Cook. He had the volumes near him in the last phase of his existence. There is a pleasant drawing representing the King in his prison, with the little Dauphin seated on his knee, pointing out the countries and oceans on a large geographical globe; and he took a pride in having had prepared "for the education of Monsieur le Dauphin," a History of the Exploration of the South Seas. It was published in Paris, in three small volumes, in 1791.

The study of Cook made a deep impression on the King's mind. Why, he asked himself, should not France share in the glory of discovering new lands, and penetrating untraversed seas? There was a large amount of exploratory work still to be done. English navigators were always busy sailing to unknown parts, but the entire world was by no means revealed yet. There were, particularly, big blank spaces at the bottom of the globe. That country called by the Dutch New Holland, the eastern part of which Cook had found — there was evidently much to be done there. What were the southern coasts like? Was it one big island-continent, or was it divided into two by a strait running south from the head of the Gulf of Carpentaria? Then there was that piece of country discovered by the Dutchman Tasman, and named Van Diemen's Land. Was it an island, or did it join on to New Holland? There were also many islands of the Pacific still to be explored and correctly charted, the map of Eastern Asia was imperfect, and the whole of the coastline of North-Western America was not accurately known.

The more Louis turned the matter over in his mind, the more he studied his globes, maps and books of voyages, the more convinced he was that France, as a maritime nation and a naval Power, ought to play an important part in this grand work of unveiling to mankind the full extent, form, nature and resources of our planet.

He sent for a man whose name the Australian reader should particularly note, because he had much to do with three important discovery voyages affecting our history. Charles Claret, Comte de Fleurieu, was the principal geographer in France. He was at this time director of ports and arsenals. He had throughout his life been a keen student of navigation, was a practical sailor, invented a marine chronometer which was a great improvement on clocks hitherto existing, devised a method of applying the metric system to the construction of marine charts, and wrote several works on his favourite subject. A large book of his on discoveries in Papua and the Solomon Islands is still of much importance.

As a French writer — an expert in this field of knowledge — has written of Fleurieu, "he it was who prepared nearly all the plans for naval operations during the war of 1778, and the instructions for the voyages of discovery — those of Laperouse and Dentrecasteaux — for which Louis XVI had given general directions; and to whose wise and well-informed advice is due in large part the utility derived from them." It was chiefly because of Fleurieu's knowledge of geography that the King chose him to be the tutor of the Dauphin; and in 1790 he became Minister of Marine.

Louis XVI and Fleurieu talked the subject over together; and the latter, at the King's command, drew up a long memorandum indicating the parts of the globe where an expedition of discovery might most profitably apply itself.

The King decided (1785) that a voyage should be undertaken; two ships of the navy, LA BOUSSOLE and L'ASTROLABE, were selected for the purpose; and, on the recommendation of the Marquis de Castries—remember Madame la Marquise!—Laperouse was chosen for the command.

All three of the men who ordered, planned and executed the voyage, the King, the scholar, and the officer, were devoted students of the work and writings of Cook; and copies of his VOYAGES, in French and English, were placed in the library of navigation carried on board the ships for the edification of the officers and crews. Over and over again in the instructions prepared—several times on a page in some places—appear references to what Cook had done, and to what Cook had left to be done; showing that both King Louis and Fleurieu knew his voyages and charts, not merely as casual readers, but intimately. As for Laperouse himself, his admiration of Cook has already been mentioned; here it may be added that when, before he sailed, Sir Joseph Banks presented him with two magnetic needles that had been used by Cook, he wrote that he "received them with feelings bordering almost upon religious veneration for the memory of that great and incomparable navigator." So that, we see, the extent of our great sailor's influence is not to be measured even by his discoveries and the effect of his writings upon his own countrymen. He radiated a magnetic force which penetrated far; down to our own day it has by no means lost its stimulating energy.

In the picture gallery at the Palace of Versailles, there is an oil painting by Mansiau, a copy of which may be seen in the Mitchell Library, Sydney. It is called "Louis XVI giving instructions to Monsieur de Laperouse for his voyage around the world." An Australian statesman who saw it during a visit to Paris a few years ago, confessed publicly on his return to his own country that he gazed long upon it, and recognised it as being "of the deepest interest to Australians." So indeed it is. A photograph of the picture is given here.

The instructions were of course prepared by Fleurieu: anyone familiar with his writings can see plenty of internal evidence of that. But Louis was not a little vain of his own geographical knowledge, and he gave a special audience to Laperouse, explaining the instructions verbally before handing them to him in writing.

They are admirably clear instructions, indicating a full knowledge of the work of preceding navigators and of the parts of the earth where discovery needed to be pursued. Their defect was that they expected too much to be done on one voyage. Let us glance over them, devoting particular attention to the portions affecting Australasia.

The ships were directed to sail across the Atlantic and round Cape Horn, visiting certain specified places on the way. In the Pacific they were to visit Easter Island, Tahiti, the Society Islands, the Friendly and Navigator groups, and New Caledonia. "He will pass Endeavour Strait and in this passage will try to ascertain whether the land of Louisiade (the Louisiade Archipelago), be contiguous to that of New Guinea, and will reconnoitre all this part of the coast from Cape Deliverance to the Island of St. Barthelomew, east-northeast of Cape Walsh, of which at present we have a very imperfect knowledge. It is much to be wished that he may be able to examine the Gulf of Carpentaria."

He was then to explore the western shores of New Holland. "He will run down the western coast and take a closer view of the southern, the greater part of which has never been visited, finishing his survey at Van Diemen's Land, at Adventure Bay or Prince Frederick Henry's, whence he will make sail for Cook's Strait, and anchor in Queen Charlotte's Sound, in that Strait, between the two islands which constitute New Zealand."

That direction is especially important, because if Laperouse had not perished, but had lived to carry out his programme, it is evident that he would have forestalled the later discoveries of Bass and Flinders in southern Australia. What a vast difference to the later course of history that might have made!

After leaving New Zealand he was to cross the Pacific to the north-west coast of America. The programme included explorations in the China Sea, at the Philippines, the Moluccas and Timor, and contemplated a return to France in July or August, 1789, after a voyage of about three years.

But although his course was mapped out in such detail, discretion was left to Laperouse to vary it if he thought fit. "All the calculations of which a sketch is given here must be governed by the circumstances of the voyage, the condition of the crews, ships and provisions, the events that may occur in the expedition and accidents which it is impossible to foresee. His Majesty, therefore, relying on the experience and judgment of the sieur de Laperouse, authorises him to make any deviation that he may deem necessary, in unforeseen cases, pursuing, however, as far as possible, the plan traced out, and conforming to the directions given in the other parts of the present instructions."

A separate set of instructions had regard to observations to be made by Laperouse upon the political conditions, possibilities of commerce, and suitability for settlement, of the lands visited by him. In the Pacific, he was to inquire "whether the cattle, fowls, and other animals which Captain Cook left on some of the islands have bred." He was to examine attentively "the north and west coasts of New Holland, and particularly that part of the coast which, being situated in the torrid zone, may enjoy some of the productions peculiar to countries in similar latitudes." In New Zealand he was to ascertain "whether the English have formed or entertain the project of forming any settlement on these islands; and if he should hear that they have actually formed a settlement, he will endeavour to repair thither in order to learn the condition, strength and object of the settlement."

It is singular that the instructions contain no reference to Botany Bay. It was the visit paid by Laperouse to this port that brought him into touch with Australian history. Yet his call there was made purely in the exercise of his discretion. He was not directed to pay any attention to eastern Australia. When he sailed the French Government knew nothing of the contemplated settlement of New South Wales by the British; and he only heard of it in the course of his voyage. Indeed, it is amazing how little was known of Australia at the time. "We have nothing authentic or sufficiently minute respecting this part of the largest island on the globe," said the instructions concerning the northern and western coasts; but there was not a word about the eastern shores.

The reader who reflects upon the facts set forth in this chapter will realise that the French Revolution, surprising as the statement may seem, affected Australian history in a remarkable way. If Louis XVI had not been dethroned and beheaded, but had remained King of France, there cannot be any doubt that he would have persisted in the investigation of the South Seas. He was deeply interested in the subject, very well informed about it, and ambitious that his country should be a great maritime and colonising Power. But the Revolution slew Louis, plunged France in long and disastrous wars, and brought Napoleon to the front. The whole course of history was diverted. It was as if a great river had been turned into a fresh channel.

If the navigator of the French King had discovered southern Australia, and settlement had followed, it is not to be supposed that Great Britain would have opposed the plans of France; for Australia then was not the Australia that we know, and England had very little use even for the bit she secured. Unthinking people might suppose that the French Revolution meant very little to us. Indeed, unthinking people are very apt to suppose that we can go our own way without regarding what takes place elsewhere. They do not realise that the world is one, and that the policies of nations interact upon each other. In point of fact, the Revolution meant a great deal to Australia. This country is, indeed, an island far from Europe, but the threads of her history are entwined with those of European history in a very curious and often intricate fashion. The French Revolution and the era of Napoleon, if we understand their consequences, really concern us quite as much as, say, the gold discoveries and the accomplishment of Federation.

Chapter V.

THE EARLY PART OF THE VOYAGE.

The expedition sailed from Brest rather sooner than had at first been contemplated, on August 1, 1785, and doubled Cape Horn in January of the following year. Some weeks were spent on the coast of Chili; and the remarks of Laperouse concerning the manners of the Spanish rulers of the country cover some of his most entertaining pages. He has an eye for the picturesque, a kindly feeling for all well-disposed people, a pleasant touch in describing customs, and shrewd judgment in estimating character. These qualities make him an agreeable writer of travels. They are fairly illustrated by the passages in which he describes the people of the city of Concepcion. Take his account of the ladies:

"The dress of these ladies, extremely different from what we have been accustomed to see, consists of a plaited petticoat, tied considerably below the waist; stockings striped red, blue and white; and shoes so short that the toes are bent under the ball of the foot so as to make it appear nearly round. Their hair is without powder and is divided into small braids behind, hanging over the shoulders. Their bodice is generally of gold or silver stuff, over which there are two short cloaks, that underneath of muslin and the other of wool of different colours, blue, yellow and pink. The upper one is drawn over the head when they are in the streets and the weather is cold; but within doors it is usual to place it on their knees; and there is a game played with the muslin cloak by continually shifting it about, in which the ladies of Concepcion display considerable grace. They are for the most part handsome, and of so polite and pleasing manners that there is certainly no maritime town in Europe where strangers are received with so much attention and kindness."

At this city Laperouse met the adventurous Irishman, Ambrose O'Higgins, who by reason of his conspicuous military abilities became commander of the Spanish forces in Chili, and afterwards Viceroy of Peru. His name originally was simply Higgins, but he prefixed the "O" when he blossomed into a Spanish Don, "as being more aristocratic." He was the father of the still more famous Bernardo O'Higgins, "the Washington of Chili," who led the revolt against Spanish rule and became first president of the Chilian Republic in 1818. Laperouse at once conceived an attachment for O'Higgins, "a man of extraordinary activity," and one "adored in the country."

In April, 1786, the expedition was at Easter Island, where the inhabitants appeared to be a set of cunning and hypocritical thieves, who "robbed us of everything which it was possible for them to carry off." Steering north, the Sandwich Islands were reached early in May. Here Laperouse liked the people, "though my prejudices were strong against them on account of the death of Captain Cook." A passage in the commander's narrative gives his opinion on the annexation of the countries of native races by Europeans, and shows that, in common with very many of his countrymen, he was much influenced by the ideas of Rousseau, then an intellectual force in France—

"Though the French were the first who, in modern times, had landed on the island of Mowee, I did not think it my duty to take possession in the name of the King. The customs of Europeans on such occasions are completely ridiculous. Philosophers must lament to see that men, for no better reason than because they are in possession of firearms and bayonets, should have no regard for the rights of sixty thousand of their fellow creatures, and should consider as an object of conquest a land fertilised by the painful exertions of its inhabitants, and for many ages the tomb of their ancestors. These islands have fortunately been discovered at a period when religion no longer serves as a pretext for violence and rapine. Modern navigators have no other object in describing the manners of remote nations than that of completing the history of man; and the knowledge they endeavour to diffuse has for its sole aim to render the people they visit more happy, and to augment their means of subsistence."

If Laperouse could see the map of the Pacific to-day he would find its groups of islands all enclosed within coloured rings, indicating possession by the great Powers of the world. He would be puzzled and pained by the change. But the history of the political movements leading to the parcelling out of seas and lands among strong States would interest him, and he would realise that the day of feeble isolation has gone. Nothing would make him marvel more than the floating of the Stars and Stripes over Hawaii, for he knew that flag during the American War of Independence. It was adopted as the flag of the United States in 1777, and during the campaign the golden lilies of the standard of France fluttered from many masts in co-operation with it. Truly a century and a quarter has brought about a wonderful change, not only in the face of the globe and in the management of its affairs, but still more radically in the ideas of men and in the motives that sway their activities!

The geographical work done by Laperouse in this part of the Pacific was of much importance. It removed from the chart five or six islands which had no existence, having been marked down erroneously by previous navigators. From this region the expedition sailed to Alaska, on the north-west coast of North America. Cook had explored here "with that courage and perseverance of which all Europe knows him to have been capable," wrote Laperouse, never failing to use an opportunity of expressing admiration for his illustrious predecessor. But there was still useful work to do, and the French occupied their time very profitably with it from June to August. Then their ships sailed down the western coast of America to California, struck east across the Pacific to the Ladrones, and made for Macao in China — then as now a Portugese possession — reaching that port in January, 1787.

The Philippines were next visited, and Laperouse formed pleasant impressions of Manilla. It is clear from his way of alluding to the customs of the Spanish inhabitants that the French captain was not a tobacco smoker. It was surprising to him that "their passion for smoking this narcotic is so immoderate that there is not an instant of the day in which either a man or woman is without a cigar;" and it is equally surprising to us that the French editor of the history of the voyage found it necessary to explain in a footnote that a cigar is "a small roll of tobacco which is smoked without the assistance of a pipe." But cigars were then little known in Europe, except among sailors and travellers who had visited the Spanish colonies; and the very spelling of the word was not fixed. In English voyages it appears as "seegar," "segar," and "sagar."

Formosa was visited in April, northern Japan in May, and the investigation of the north-eastern coasts of Asia occupied until October.

A passage in a letter from Laperouse to Fleurieu is worth quoting for two reasons. It throws some light on the difficulties of navigation in unknown seas, and upon the commander's severe application to duty; and it also serves to remind us that Japan, now so potent a factor in the politics of the East and of the whole Pacific, had not then emerged from the barbarian exclusiveness towards foreigners, which she had maintained since Europe commenced to exploit Asia. In the middle of the seventeenth century she had expelled the Spaniards and the Portugese with much bloodshed, and had closed her ports to all traders except the Chinese and the Dutch, who were confined to a prescribed area at Nagasaki. Intercourse with all other foreign peoples was strictly forbidden. Even as late as 1842 it was commanded that if any foreign vessel were driven by distress or tempestuous weather into a Japanese port, she might only remain so long as was necessary to meet her wants, and must then depart. Laperouse knew of this jealous Japanese antipathy to foreign visitors, and, as he explains in the letter, meant to keep away from the country because of it. He wrote: —

"The part of our voyage between Manilla and Kamchatka will afford you, I hope, complete satisfaction. It was the newest, the most interesting, and certainly, from the everlasting fogs which enveloped the land in the latitudes we traversed, the most difficult. These fogs are such that it has taken one hundred and fifty days to explore a part of the coast which Captain King, in the third volume of Cook's last voyage, supposes might be examined in the course of two months. During this period I rested only ten days, three in the Bay of Ternai, two in the Bay de Langle, and five in the Bay de Castries. Thus I wasted no time; I even forebore to circumnavigate the island of Chicha (Yezo) by traversing the Strait of Sangaar (Tsugaru). I should have wished to anchor, if possible, at the northern point of Japan, and would perhaps have ventured to send a boat ashore, though such a proceeding would have required the most serious deliberation, as the boat would probably have been stopped. Where a merchant ship is concerned an event of this kind might be considered as of little importance, but the seizure of a boat belonging to a ship of war could scarcely be otherwise regarded than as a national insult; and the taking and burning of a few sampans would be a very sorry compensation as against the people who would not exchange a single European of whom they were desirous of making an example, for one hundred Japanese. I was, however, too far from the coast to include such an intention, and it is impossible for me to judge at present what I should have done had the contrary been the case.

"It would be difficult for me to find words to express to you the fatigue attending this part of my voyage, during which I did not once undress myself, nor did a single night pass without my being obliged to spend several hours upon deck. Imagine to yourself six days of fog with only two or three hours of clear weather, in seas extremely confined, absolutely unknown, and where fancy, in con-sequence of the information we had received, pictured to us shoals and currents that did not always exist. From the place where we made the land on the eastern coast of Tartary, to the strait which we discovered between Tchoka (Saghalien) and Chicha, we did not fail to take the bearing of every point, and you may rest assured that neither creek, port, nor river escaped our attention, and that many charts, even of the coasts of Europe, are less exact than those which we shall bring with us on our return."

"The strait which we discovered" is still called Laperouse Strait on most modern maps, though the Japanese usually call it Soya Strait. It runs between Yezo, the large northerly island of Japan, and Sa-ghalien. Current maps also show the name Boussole Strait, after Laperouse's ship, between Urup and Simusir, two of the Kurile chain of small islands curving from Yezo to the thumblike extremity of Kamchatka.

At Petropavlovsk in Kamchatka the drawings of the artists and the journals of the commander up to date were packed up, and sent to France overland across Asiatic Russia, in charge of a young member of the staff, J. B. B. de Lesseps. He was the only one of the expedition who ever returned to Europe. By not coming to Australia he saved his life. He published a book about his journey, a remark-able feat of land travel in those days. He was the uncle of a man whose remarkable engineering work has made Australia's relations with Europe much easier and more speedy than they were in earlier years: that Ferdinand de Lesseps who (1859-69) planned and carried out the construction of the Suez Canal. The ships, after replenishing, sailed for the south Pacific, where we shall follow the proceedings of Laperouse in rather closer detail than has been considered necessary in regard to the American and Asiatic phases of the voyage.

Chapter VI.

LAPEROUSE IN THE PACIFIC.

On the 6th December, 1787, the expedition made the eastern end of the Navigator Islands, that is, the Samoan Group. As the ships approached, a party of natives were observed squatting under cocoanut trees. Presently sixteen canoes put off from the land, and their occupants, after paddling round the vessels distrustfully, ventured to approach and proffer cocoanuts in exchange for strings of beads and strips of red cloth. The natives got the better of the bargain, for, when they had received their price, they hurried off without delivering their own goods. Further on, an old chief delivered an harangue from the shore, holding a branch of Kava in his hand. "We knew from what we had read of several voyages that it was a token of peace; and throwing him some pieces of cloth we answered by the word 'TAYO,' which signified 'friend' in the dialect of the South Sea Islands; but we were not sufficiently experienced to understand and pronounce distinctly the words of the vocabularies we had extracted from Cook."

Nearly all the early navigators made a feature of compiling vocabularies of native words, and Cook devoted particular care to this task. Dr. Walter Roth, formerly protector of Queensland aboriginals a trained observer, has borne testimony as recently as last year (in THE TIMES, December 29, 1911) that a list of words collected from Endeavour Strait blacks, and "given by Captain Cook, are all more or less recognisable at the present day." But Cook's spellings were intended to be pronounced in the English mode. Laperouse and his companions by giving the vowels French values would hardly be likely to make the English navigator's vocabularies intelligible.

The native canoes amused the French captain. They "could be of use only to people who are expert swimmers, for they are constantly turned over. This is an accident, however, at which they feel less surprise and anxiety than we should at a hat's blowing off. They lift the canoe on their shoulders, and after they have emptied it of the water, get into it again, well assured that they will have the same operation to perform within half an hour, for it is as difficult to preserve a balance in these ticklish things as to dance upon a rope."

At Mauna Island (now called Tutuila) some successful bargaining was done with glass beads in exchange for pork and fruits. It surprised Laperouse that the natives chose these paltry ornaments rather than hatchets and tools. "They preferred a few beads which could be of no utility, to anything we could offer them in iron or cloth."

Two days later a tragedy occurred at this island, when Captain de Langle, the commander of the ASTROLABE, and eleven of the crew were murdered. He made an excursion inland to look for fresh water, and found a clear, cool spring in the vicinity of a village. The ships were not urgently in need of water, but de Langle "had embraced the system of Cook, and thought fresh water a hundred times preferable to what had been some time in the hold. As some of his crew had slight symptoms of scurvy, he thought, with justice, that we owed them every means of alleviation in our power. Besides, no island could be compared with this for abundance of provisions. The two ships had already procured upwards of 500 hogs, with a large quantity of fowls, pigeons and fruits; and all these had cost us only a few beads."

Laperouse himself doubted the prudence of sending a party inland, as he had observed signs of a turbulent spirit among the islanders. But de Langle insisted on the desirableness of obtaining fresh water where it was abundant, and "replied to me that my refusal would render me responsible for the progress of the scurvy, which began to appear with some violence." He undertook to go at the head of the party, and, relying on his judgment, the commander consented.

Two boats left the ship at about noon, and landed their casks undisturbed. But when the party returned they found a crowd of over a thousand natives assembled, and a dangerous disposition soon revealed itself amongst them. It is possible that the Frenchmen had, unconsciously, offended against some of their superstitious rites. Certainly they had not knowingly been provoked. They had peacefully bartered their fruits and nuts for beads, and had been treated in a friendly fashion throughout. But the currents of passion that sweep through the minds of savage peoples baffle analysis. Something had disturbed them; what it was can hardly be surmised. One of the officers believed that the gift of some beads to a few, excited the envy of the others. It may be so; mere envy plays such a large part in the affairs even of civilised peoples, that we need not wonder to find it arousing the anger of savages. Laperouse tells what occurred in these terms: —

"Several canoes, after having sold their ladings of provisions on board our ships, had returned ashore, and all landed in this bay, so that it was gradually filled. Instead of two hundred persons, including women and children, whom M. de Langle found when he arrived at half past one, there were ten or twelve hundred by three o'clock. He succeeded in embarking his water; but the bay was by this time nearly dry, and he could not hope to get his boats afloat before four o'clock, when the tide would have risen. He stepped into them, however, with his detachment, and posted himself in the bow, with his musket and his marines, forbidding them to fire unless he gave orders.

"This, he began to realise, he would soon be forced to do. Stones flew about, and the natives, only up to the knees in water, surrounded the boats within less than three yards. The marines who were in the boats, attempted in vain to keep them off. If the fear of commencing hostilities and being accused of barbarity had not checked M. de Langle, he would unquestionably have ordered a general discharge of his swivels and musketry, which no doubt would have dispersed the mob, but he flattered himself that he could check them without shedding blood, and he fell a victim to his humanity.

"Presently a shower of stones thrown from a short distance with as much force as if they had come from a sling, struck almost every man in the boat. M. de Langle had only time to discharge the two barrels of his piece before he was knocked down; and unfortunately he fell over the larboard bow of the boat, where upwards of two hundred natives instantly massacred him with clubs and stones. When he was dead, they made him fast by the arm to one of the tholes of the long boat, no doubt to secure his spoil. The BOUS-SOLE'S long-boat, commanded by M. Boutin, was aground within four yards of the ASTROLABE'S, and parallel with her, so as to leave a little channel between them, which was unoccupied by the natives. Through this all the wounded men, who were so fortunate as not to fall on the other side of the boats, escaped by swimming to the barges, which, happily remaining afloat, were enabled to save forty-nine men out of the sixty-one."

Amongst the wounded was Pere Receveur, priest, naturalist and shoemaker, who later on died of his injuries at Botany Bay, and whose tomb there is as familiar as the Laperouse monument.

The anger of the Frenchmen at the treachery of the islanders was not less than their grief at the loss of their companions. Laperouse, on the first impulse, was inclined to send a strongly-armed party ashore to avenge the massacre. But two of the officers who had escaped pointed out that in the cove where the incident occurred the trees came down almost to the sea, affording shelter to the natives, who would be able to shower stones upon the party, whilst themselves remaining beyond reach of musket balls.

"It was not without difficulty," he wrote, "that I could tear myself away from this fatal place, and leave behind the bodies of our murdered companions. I had lost an old friend; a man of great understanding, judgment, and knowledge; and one of the best officers in the French navy. His humanity had occasioned his death. Had he but allowed himself to fire on the first natives who entered into the water to surround the boats, he would have prevented his own death as well as those of eleven other victims of savage ferocity. Twenty persons more were severely wounded; and this event deprived us for the time of thirty men, and the only two boats we had large enough to carry a sufficient number of men, armed, to attempt a descent. These considerations determined my subsequent conduct. The slightest loss would have compelled me to burn one of my ships in order to man the other. If my anger had required only the death of a few natives, I had had an opportunity after the massacre of sinking and destroying a hundred canoes containing upwards of five hundred persons, but I was afraid of being mistaken in my victims, and the voice of my conscience saved their lives."

It was then that Laperouse resolved to sail to Botany Bay, of which he had read a description in Cook's Voyages. His long-boats had been destroyed by the natives, but he had on board the frames of two new ones, and a safe anchorage was required where they could be put together. His crews were exasperated; and lest there should be a collision between them and other natives he resolved that, while reconnoitring other groups of islands to determine their correct latitude, he would not permit his sailors to land till he reached Botany Bay. There he knew that he could obtain wood and water.

On December 14 Oyolava (now called Upolu) was reached. Here again the ships were surrounded by canoes, and the angry French sailors would have fired upon them except for the positive orders of their commander. Throughout this unfortunate affair the strict sense of justice, which forbade taking general vengeance for the misdeeds of particular people, stands out strongly in the conduct of Laperouse. He acknowledged in letters written from Botany Bay, that in future relations with uncivilised folk he would adopt more repressive measures, as experience taught him that lack of firm handling was by them regarded as weakness. But his tone in all his writings is humane and kindly.

The speculations of Laperouse concerning the origin of these peoples, are interesting, and deserve consideration by those who speak and write upon the South Seas. He was convinced that they are all derived from an ancient common stock, and that the race of woolly-haired men to be found in the interior of Formosa were the far-off parents of the natives of the Philippines, Papua, New Britain, the New Hebrides, the Friendly Islands, the Carolines, Ladrones, and Sandwich Groups. He believed that in those islands the interior of which did not afford complete shelter the original inhabitants were conquered by Malays, after which aboriginals and invaders mingled together, producing modifications of the original types. But in Papua, the Solomons and the New Hebrides, the Malays made little impression. He accounted for differences in appearance amongst the people of the islands he visited by the different degrees of Malay intermixture, and believed that the very black people found on some islands, "whose complexion still remains a few shades deeper than that of certain families in the same islands" were to be accounted for by certain families making it "a point of honour not to contaminate their blood." The theory is at all events striking. We have a "White Australia policy" on the mainland to-day; this speculation assumes a kind of "Black Australasia policy" on the part of certain families of islanders from time immemorial.

The Friendly Islands were reached in December, but the commander had few and unimportant relations with them. On the 13th January, 1788, the ships made for Norfolk Island, and came to anchor opposite the place where Cook was believed to have landed. The sea was running high at the time, breaking violently on the rocky shores of the north east. The naturalists desired to land to collect specimens, but the heavy breakers prevented them. The commander permitted them to coast along the shore in boats for about half a league but then recalled them.

"Had it been possible to land, there was no way of getting into the interior part of the island but by ascending for thirty or forty yards the rapid stream of some torrents, which had formed gullies. Beyond these natural barriers the island was covered with pines and carpeted with the most beautiful verdure. It is probable that we should then have met with some culinary vegetables, and this hope increased our desire of visiting a land where Captain Cook had landed with the greatest facility. He, it is true, was here in fine weather, that had continued for several days; whilst we had been sailing in such heavy seas that for eight day, our ports had been shut and our dead-lights in. From the ship I watched the motions of the boats with my glass; and seeing, as night approached, that they had found no convenient place for landing, I made the signal to recall them, and soon after gave orders for getting under way. Perhaps I should have lost much time had I waited for a more favourable opportunity: and the exploring of this island was not worth such a sacrifice."

At eight in the evening the ships got under way, and at day-break on the following morning sail was crowded for Botany Bay.

Chapter VII.

AT BOTANY BAY.

When, in 1787, the British Government entrusted Captain Arthur Phillip with a commission to establish a colony at Botany Bay, New South Wales, they gave him explicit directions as to where he should locate the settlement. "According to the best information which we have obtained," his instructions read, "Botany Bay appears to be the most eligible situation upon the said coast for the first establishment, possessing a commodious harbour and other advantages which no part of the said coast hitherto discovered affords." But Phillip was a trustworthy man who, in so serious a matter as the choice of a site for a town, did not follow blindly the commands of respectable elderly gentlemen thousands of miles away. It was his business to found a settlement successfully. To do that he must select the best site.

After examining Botany Bay, he decided to take a trip up the coast and see if a better situation could not be found. On the 21st January, 1788, he entered Port Jackson with three boats, and found there "the finest harbour in the world, in which a thousand sail of the line may ride in the most perfect security." He fixed upon a cove "which I honoured with the name of Sydney." and decided that that was there he would "plant." Every writer of mediaeval history who has had occasion to refer to the choice by Constantine the Great of Byzantium, afterwards Constantinople, as his capital, has extolled his judgment and prescience. Constantine was an Emperor, and could do as he would. Arthur Phillip was an official acting under orders. We can never sufficiently admire the wisdom he displayed when, exercising his own discretion, he decided upon Port Jackson. True, he had a great opportunity, but his signal merit is that he grasped it when it was presented, that he gave more regard to the success of his task than to the letter of his instructions.

While he was making the search, the eleven vessels composing the First Fleet lay in Botany Bay. He returned on the evening of the 23rd, and immediately gave orders that the whole company should as soon as possible sail for Port Jackson, declaring it to be, in King's quaint words, "a very proper place to form an establisht. in."

To the great astonishment of the Fleet, on the 24th, two strange ships made their appearance to the south of Solander Point, a projection from the peninsula on which now stands the obelisk in memory of Cook's landing. What could they be? Some guessed that they were English vessels with additional stores. Some supposed that they were Dutch, "coming after us to oppose our landing." Nobody expected to see any ships in these untraversed waters, and we can easily picture the amazement of officers, crews, and convicts when the white sails appeared. The more timid speculated on the possibility of attack, and there were "temporary apprehensions, accompanied by a multiplicity of conjectures, many of them sufficiently ridiculous."

Phillip, however, remembered hearing that the French had an expedition of discovery either in progress or contemplation. He was the first to form a right opinion about them, but, wishing to be certain, sent the SUPPLY out of the bay to get a nearer view and hoist the British colours. Lieutenant Ball, in command of that brig, after reconnoitring, reported that the ships were certainly not English. They were either French, Spanish or Portuguese. He could distinctly see the white field of the flag they flew, "but they were at too great a distance to discover if there was anything else on it." The flag, of course, showed the golden lilies of France on a white ground. One of the ships, King records, "wore a CHEF D'ESCADRE'S pennant," that is, a commodore's.

This information satisfied Phillip, who was anxious to lose no time in getting his people ashore at Sydney Cove. He, therefore, determined to sail in the SUPPLY on the 25th, to make preliminary arrangements, leaving Captain Hunter of the SIRIUS to convoy the Fleet round as soon as possible. The wind, just then, was blowing too strong for them to work out of the Bay.

Meanwhile, Laperouse, with the BOUSSOLE and the ASTROLABE, was meeting with heavy weather in his attempt to double Point Solander. The wind blew hard from that quarter, and his ships were too heavy sailers to force their passage against wind and current combined. The whole of the 24th was spent in full sight of Botany Bay, which they could not enter. But their hearts were cheered by the spectacle of the pennants and ensigns on the eleven

British vessels, plainly seen at intervals within, and the prospect of meeting Europeans again made them impatient to fetch their anchorage.

The SIRIUS was just about to sail when the French vessels entered the Bay at nine in the morning of January 26, but Captain Hunter courteously sent over a lieutenant and midshipman, with his compliments and offers of such assistance as it was in his power to give. "I despatched an officer," records Laperouse, "to return my thanks to Captain Hunter, who by this time had his anchor a-peak and his topsails hoisted, telling him that my wants were confined to wood and water, of which we could not fail in this Bay; and I was sensible that vessels intended to settle a colony at such a distance from Europe could not be of any assistance to navigators." The English lieutenant, according to Laperouse, "appeared to make a great mystery of Commodore Phillip's plan, and we did not take the liberty of putting any questions to him on the subject." It was not the business of a junior officer to give unauthorised information, but perhaps his manner made a greater mystery of the Governor's plans than the circumstances required.

It was at Kamchatka that the French had learnt that the British were establishing a settlement in New South Wales; but Laperouse, when he arrived at Botany Bay, had no definite idea as to the progress they had made. According to Lieutenant-Colonel Paterson, he expected to find a town built and a market established. Instead of that he found the first colonists abandoning the site where it was originally intended that they should settle, and preparing to fix their abode at another spot. But after he had seen something of Botany Bay he expressed himself as "convinced of the propriety and absolute necessity of the measure."

The later relations between the English and French were of the most pleasant kind. It does not appear from the writings of those who have left records that Phillip and Laperouse ever met, or that the latter ever saw the beginnings of Sydney. His ships certainly never entered Port Jackson. But we learn from Captain Tench that "during their stay in the port" (i.e. in Botany Bay) "the officers of the two nations had frequent opportunities of testifying their mutual regard by visits and other interchanges of friendship and esteem;"

and Laperouse gratified the English especially "by the feeling manner in which he always mentioned the name and talents of Captain Cook."

Not only in what he wrote with an eye to publication, but in his private correspondence, Laperouse expressed his gratification at the friendly relations established. He spoke of "frequent intercourse" with the English, and said that "to the most polite attentions they have added every offer of service in their power; and it was not without regret that we saw them depart, almost immediately upon our arrival, for Port Jackson, fifteen miles to the northward of this place. Commodore Phillip had good reason to prefer that port, and he has left us sole masters of this bay, where our long-boats are already on the stocks."

The fullest account is given in the journal of Lieutenant King, afterwards (1800-6) Governor of New South Wales. On February 1 Phillip sent him in a cutter, in company with Lieutenant Dawes of the Marines, to visit Laperouse, "and to offer him whatever he might have occasion for." King relates that they were "received with the greatest politeness and attention by Monsieur de Laperouse and his officers." He accepted an invitation to remain during the day with the French, to dine with the Commodore, and to return to Port Jackson next morning. The complete history of the voyage was narrated to him, including of course the tragic story of the massacre of de Langle and his companions.

After dinner on the BOUSSOLE, King was taken ashore, where he found the French "quite established, having thrown round their tents a stockade, guarded by two small guns." This defence was needed to protect the frames of the two new longboats, which were being put together, from the natives; and also, it would appear, from a few escaped convicts, "whom he had dismissed with threats, giving them a day's provision to carry them back to ye settlement." Laperouse himself, in his history—in the very last words of it, in fact—complains that "we had but too frequent opportunities of hearing news of the English settlement, the deserters from which gave us a great deal of trouble and embarrassment."

We learn from King a little about the Pere Receveur—a very little, truly, but sufficient to make us wish to know more. From the circumstance that his quarters were on the ASTROLABE, and that, therefore, he was not brought very much under the notice of Laperouse, we read scarcely anything about him in the commander's book. Once during the voyage some acids used by him for scientific purposes ignited, and set fire to the ship, but the danger was quickly suppressed. This incident, and that of the wounding of Receveur at Manua, are nearly all we are told about him from the commander. But he struck King as being "a man of letters and genius." He was a collector of natural curiosities, having under his care "a great number of philosophical instruments." King's few lines, giving the impression derived from a necessarily brief conversation, seem to bring the Abbe before us in a flash. "A man of letters and genius": how gladly we would know more of one of whom those words could be written! Receveur died shortly before Laperouse sailed away, and was buried at the foot of a tree, to which were nailed a couple of boards bearing an inscription. Governor Phillip, when the boards fell down, had the inscription engraved on a copper plate. The tomb, which is now so prominent an object at Botany Bay, was erected by the Baron de Bougainville in 1825. The memorials to the celebrated navigator and the simple scholar stand together.

King, in common with Tench, records the admiring way in which Laperouse spoke of Cook. He "informed me that every place where he has touched or been near, he found all the astronomical and nautical works of Captain Cook to be very exact and true, and concluded by saying, 'Enfin, Monsieur Cook a tant fait qu'il ne m'a rien laisse a faire que d' admirer ses oeuvres.'" (In short, Mr. Cook has done so much that he has left me nothing to do but to admire his works).

There is very little more to tell about those few weeks spent at Botany Bay before the navigator and his companions "vanished trackless into blue immensity," as Carlyle puts it. A fragment of conversation is preserved by Tench. A musket was fired one day, and the natives marvelled less at the noise than at the fact that the bullet made a hole in a piece of bark at which it was aimed. To calm them, "an officer whistled the air of 'Malbrook,' which they appeared highly charmed with, and greeted him with equal pleasure and readiness. I may remark here," adds the Captain of Marines, "what I was afterwards told by Monsieur de Perousse" (so he misspells the name) "that the natives of California, as throughout all the isles of the Pacific Ocean, and in short wherever he had been, seemed equally touched and delighted with this little plaintive air." It is gratifying to be able to record Captain Tench's high opinion of the efficacy of the tune, which is popularly known nowadays as "We won't go home till morning." One has often heard of telling things "to the Marines." This gallant officer, doubtless, used to whistle them, to a "little plaintive air."

It was the practice of Laperouse to sow seeds at places visited by his ships, with the object of experimenting with useful European plants that might be cultivated in other parts of the world. His own letters and journal do not show that he did so at Botany Bay; but we have other evidence that he did, and that the signs of cultivation had not vanished at least ten years later. When George Bass was returning to Sydney in February, 1798, at the end of that wonderful cruise in a whaleboat which had led to the discovery of Westernport, he was becalmed off Botany Bay. He was disposed to enter and remain there for the night, but his journal records that his people—the six picked British sailors who were the companions of his enterprise—"seemed inclined to push for home rather than go up to the Frenchman's Garden." Therefore, the wind failing, they took to the oars and rowed to Port Jackson, reaching home at ten o'clock at night. That is a very interesting allusion. The Frenchman's Garden must have been somewhere within the enclosed area where the Cable Station now stands, and it would be well if so pleasant a name, and one so full of historical suggestion, were still applied to that reserve.

It may be well to quote in full the passage in which Laperouse relates his experience of Botany Bay. He was not able to write his journal up to the date of his departure before despatching it to Europe, but the final paragraphs in it sufficiently describe what occurred, and what he thought. Very loose and foolish statements have occasionally been published as to his object in visiting the port. In one of the geographical journals a few years ago the author saw it stated that there was "a race for a Continent" between the English and the French, in which the former won by less than a week! Nonsense of that sort, even though it appears in sober publications, issued with a scientific purpose, can emanate only from those who have no real acquaintance with the subject. There was no race, no struggle for priority, no thought of territorial acquisition on the part of the French. The reader of this little book knows by this time that the visit to Botany Bay was not originally contemplated. It was not in the programme.

What would have happened if Laperouse had safely returned home, and if the French Revolution had not destroyed Louis XVI and blown his exploration and colonisation schemes into thin air, is quite another question; but "ifs" are not history. You can entirely reconstruct the history of the human race by using enough "ifs," but with that sort of thing, which an ironist has termed "Iftory," and is often more amusing than enlightening, more speculative than sound, we have at present nothing to do. Here is the version of the visit given by Laperouse himself: —

"We made the land on the 23rd January. It has little elevation, and is scarcely possible to be seen at a greater distance than twelve leagues. The wind then became very variable; and, like Captain Cook, we met with currents, which carried us every day fifteen minutes south of our reckoning; so that we spent the whole of the 24th in plying in sight of Botany Bay, without being able to double Point Solander, which bore from us a league north. The wind blew strong from that quarter, and our ships were too heavy sailers to surmount the force of the wind and the currents combined; but that day we had a spectacle to which we had been altogether unaccustomed since our departure from Manilla. This was a British squadron, at anchor in Botany Bay, the pennants and ensigns of which we could plainly distinguish. All Europeans are countrymen at such a distance from home, and we had the most eager impatience to fetch the anchorage; but the next day the weather was so foggy that it was impossible to discern the land, and we did not get in till the 26th, at nine in the morning, when we let go our anchor a mile from the north shore, in seven fathoms of water, on a good bottom of grey sand, abreast of the second bay.

"The moment I made my appearance in the entrance of the Bay, a lieutenant and midshipman were sent aboard my vessel by Captain Hunter, commanding the British frigate SIRIUS. They offered from him all the services in his power; adding, however, that, as he was just getting under way to proceed to the northward, circumstances would not allow him to furnish us with provision, ammunition or sails; so that his offers of service were reduced to good wishes for the future success of our voyage.

"I despatched an officer to return my thanks to Captain Hunter, who by this time had his anchor a-peak, and his topsails hoisted; telling him that my wants were confined to wood and water, of which we could not fail in this Bay; and I was sensible that vessels intended to settle a colony at such a distance from Europe, could not be of any assistance to navigators.

"From the lieutenant we learnt that the English squadron was commanded by Commodore Phillip, who had sailed from Botany Bay the previous evening in the SUPPLY, sloop, with four transports, in search of a more commodious place for a settlement further north. The lieutenant appeared to make a great mystery of Commodore Phillip's plan, and we did not take the liberty of putting any questions to him on the subject; but we had no doubt that the intended settlement must be very near Botany Bay, since several boats were under sail for the place, and the passage certainly must be very short, as it was thought unnecessary to hoist them on board. The crew of the English boat, less discreet than their officer, soon informed our people that they were only going to Port Jackson, sixteen miles north of Point Banks, where Commander Phillip had himself reconnoitred a very good harbour, which ran ten miles into the land, to the south-west, and in which the ships might anchor within pistol-shot of the shore, in water as smooth as that of a basin. We had, afterwards, but too frequent opportunities of hearing news of the English settlement, the deserters from which gave us a great deal of trouble and embarrassment."

Pieced together thus is nearly all we know about Laperouse during his visit to Botany Bay. It is not much. We would gladly have many more details. What has become of the letter he wrote to Phillip recommending (according to King) the Pacific Islands as worthy of the attention of the new colony, "for the great quantity of stock with which they abound"? Apparently it is lost. The grave and the deep have swallowed up the rest of this "strange eventful history," and we interrogate in vain. We should know even less than we do were it not that Laperouse obtained from Phillip permission to send home, by the next British ship leaving Port Jackson, his journal, some charts, and the drawings of his artists. This material, added to private letters and a few miscellaneous papers, was placed in charge of Lieutenant Shortland to be delivered to the French Ambassador in London, and formed part of the substance of the two volumes and atlas published in Paris.

It may be well to cite, as a note to this chapter, the books in which contemporary accounts of the visit of Laperouse and his ships to Botany Bay are to be found. Some readers may thereby be tempted to look into the original authorities. Laperouse's own narrative is contained in the third and fourth volumes of his "Voyage autour du Monde," edited by Milet-Mureau (Paris, 1797). There are English translations. A few letters at the end of the work give a little additional information. Governor Phillip's "Voyage to Botany Bay" (London, 1789) contains a good but brief account. Phillip's despatch to the Secretary of State, Lord Sydney, printed in the "Historical Records of New South Wales," Vol. I., part 2, p. 121, devotes a paragraph to the subject. King's Journal in Vol. II. of the "Records," p. 543-7, gives his story. Surgeon Bowes' Journal, on page 391 of the same volume, contains a rather picturesque allusion. Hunter's "Voyage to Botany Bay" (London, 1793) substantially repeats King's version. Captain Watkin Tench, of the Marines, has a good account in his "Narrative of an Expedition to Botany Bay" (London, 1789), and Paterson's "History of New South Wales" (Newcastle-on-Tyne, 1811) makes an allusion to the French expedition.

Chapter VIII.

THE MYSTERY, AND THE SECRET OF THE SEA.

The BOUSSOLE and the ASTROLABE sailed from Botany Bay on March 10, 1788. After recording that fact we might well inscribe the pathetic last words of Hamlet, "the rest is silence."

We know what Laperouse intended to do. He wrote two letters to friends in France, explaining the programme to be followed after sailing from Botany Bay. They do not agree in every particular, but we may take the last letter written to express his final determination. According to this, his plan was to sail north, passing between Papua (New Guinea) and Australia by another channel than Endeavour Strait, if he could find one. During September and October he intended to visit the Gulf of Carpentaria, and thence sail down the west and along the south of Australia, to Tasmania, "but in such a manner that it may be possible for me to stretch northward in time to arrive at Ile-de-France in the beginning of December, 1788." That was the programme which he was not destined to complete — hardly, indeed, to enter upon. Had he succeeded, his name would have been inscribed amongst the memorable company of the world's great maritime explorers. As it is, the glint on his brow, as he stands in the light of history, is less that of achievement than of high promise, noble aims, romance and mystery.

One of the letters sent from Sydney concluded with these words: "Adieu! I shall depart in good health, as are all my ship's company. We would undertake six voyages round the world if it could afford to our country either profit or pleasure." They were not the last words he wrote, but we may appropriately take them as being, not merely his adieu to a friend, but to the world.

Time sped on; the date given for the arrival at Ile-de-France was passed; the year 1789 dawned and ticked off the tally of its days. But nothing was heard of Laperouse. People in France grew anxious, one especially we may be sure — she who knew so well where the ships would anchor in Port Louis if they emerged out of the ocean brume, and who longed so ardently that renewed acquaintance with scenes once sweetly familiar would awaken memories meet to give wings to speed and spurs to delay. Not a word came to sustain or cheer, and the faint flush of hope faded to the wan hue of despair on the cheek of love. By 1791 all expectation of seeing the expedition return was abandoned. But could not some news of its fate be ascertained? Had it faded out of being like a summer cloud, leaving not a trace behind? Might not some inkling be had, some small relics obtained, some whisper caught, in those distant isles,

> "Where the sea egg flames on the coral,
>   and the long-backed breakers croon
> Their endless ocean legend to the lazy, locked lagoon."

France was then in the throes of her great social earthquake; but it stands to the credit of the National Assembly that, amidst many turbulent projects and boiling passions, they found time and had the disposition to cause the fitting out of a new expedition to search for tidings of those whose disappearance weighed heavily on the heart of the nation. The decree was passed on February 9, 1791.

Two ships, the RECHERCHE and the ESPERANCE, were selected and placed under the command of Dentrecasteaux. He had already had some experience in a part of the region to be searched, had been a governor of Ile-de-France, and during a South Sea voyage had named the cluster of islands east of Papua now called the D'Entrecasteaux Group. The second ship was placed under the command of Captain Huon Kermadec. The Huon River in Tasmania, and the Kermadec Islands, N.E. of New Zealand, are named after him.

Fleurieu again drew up the instructions, and based them largely upon the letter from Laperouse quoted above, pointing out that remains of him would most probably be found in the neighbourhood of coasts which he had intended to explore. It was especially indicated that there was, south of New Holland, an immense stretch of coastline so far utterly unknown. "No navigator has penetrated in that part of the sea; the reconnaissances and discoveries of the Dutch, the English and the French commenced at the south of Van Diemen's Land."

Thus, for the second time, was a French navigator directed to explore the southern coasts of Australia; and had Dentrecasteaux followed the plan laid down for him he would have forestalled the discoveries of Grant, Bass and Flinders, just as Laperouse would have done had his work not been cut short by disaster.

It has to be remembered that the instructions impressed upon Dentrecasteaux that his business primarily was not geographical discovery, but to get news of his lost compatriots. But even so, is it not curious that the French should have been concerned with the exploration of Southern Australia before the English thought about it; that they should have had two shots at the task, planned with knowledge and care, officially directed, and in charge of eminently competent navigators; but that nevertheless their schemes should have gone awry? They made a third attempt by means of Baudin's expedition, during the Napoleonic Consulate, and again were unsuccessful, except in a very small measure. It almost seems as if some power behind human endeavours had intended these coasts for British finding—and keeping.

The full story of Dentrecasteaux' expedition has not yet been told. Two thick books were written about it, but a mass of unpublished papers contain details that were judiciously kept out of those volumes. When the whole truth is made known, it will be seen that the bitter strife which plunged France in an agony of blood and tears was not confined to the land.

The ships did not visit Sydney. Why not? It might have been expected that an expedition sent to discover traces of Laperouse would have been careful to make Botany Bay in the first instance, and, after collecting whatever evidence was available there, would have carefully followed the route that he had proposed to pursue. But it would seem that an European settlement was avoided. Why? The unpublished papers may furnish an answer to that question.

Neither was the south coast of Australia explored. That great chance was missed. Some excellent charting—which ten years later commanded the cordial admiration of Flinders—was done by Beautemps-Beaupre, who was Dentrecasteaux' cartographer, especially round about the S.W. corner of the continent. Esperance Bay, in Western Australia, is named after one of the ships of this expedition. But from that corner, his ships being short of fresh water, Dentrecasteaux sailed on a direct line to Southern Tasmania, and thence to New Zealand, New Caledonia, and New Guinea. Touch with the only European centre in these parts was—apparently with deliberation—not obtained.

Dentrecasteaux died while his ships were in the waters to the north of New Guinea. He fell violently ill, raving at first, then subsiding into unconsciousness, a death terrible to read about in the published narrative, where the full extent of his troubles is not revealed. Kermadec, commander of the ESPERANCE, also died at New Caledonia. After their decease the ships returned to France as rapidly as they could. They were detained by the Dutch at Sourabaya for several months, as prisoners of war, and did not reach Europe till March, 1796. Their mission had been abortive.

Five French Captains who brought expeditions to Australia at this period all ended in misfortune. Laperouse was drowned; de Langle was murdered; Dentrecasteaux died miserably at sea; Kermadec, the fourth, had expired shortly before; and Baudin, the fifth, died at Port Louis on the homeward voyage.

Nor is even that the last touch of melancholy to the tale of tragedy. There was a young poet who was touched by the fate of Laperouse. Andre Chenier is now recognised as one of the finest masters of song who have enriched French literature, and his poems are more and more studied and admired both by his own countrymen and abroad. He planned and partly finished a long poem, "L'Amerique," which contains a mournful passage about the mystery of the sea which had not then been solved. A translation of the lines will not be attempted here; they are mentioned because the poet himself had an end as tragic, though in a different mode, as that of the hero of whom he sang. He came under the displeasure of the tyrants of the Red Terror through his friends and his writings, and in March, 1794, the guillotine took this brilliant young genius as a victim.

> J'accuserai les vents et cette mer jalouse
> Qui retient, qui peut-etre a ravi Laperouse

so the poem begins. How strangely the shadow of Tragedy hangs over this ill-starred expedition; Louis XVI the projector, Laperouse and de Langle the commanders, Dentrecasteaux and Kermadec the searchers, Andre Chenier the laureate: the breath of the black-robed Fury was upon them all!

Chapter IX.

CAPTAIN DILLON'S DISCOVERY.

The navigators of all nations were fascinated by the mystery attaching to the fate of Laperouse. Every ship that sailed the Pacific hoped to obtain tidings or remains. From time to time rumours arose of the discovery of relics. One reported the sight of wreckage; another that islanders had been seen dressed in French uniforms; another that a cross of St. Louis had been found. But the element of probability in the various stories evaporated on investigation. Flinders, sailing north from Port Jackson in the INVESTIGATOR in 1802, kept a sharp lookout on the Barrier Reef, the possibility of finding some trace being "always present to my mind." But no definite news came.

A new French voyage of exploration came down to the Pacific in 1817, under the command of Louis de Freycinet, who had been a lieutenant in Baudin's expedition in 1800-4. The purpose was not chiefly to look for evidence concerning Laperouse, though naturally a keen scrutiny was maintained with this object in view.

An extremely queer fact may be mentioned in connection with this voyage. The URANIE carried a woman among the crew, the only one of her sex amidst one hundred men. Madame de Freycinet, the wife of the commandant, joined at Toulon, dressed as a ship's boy, and it was given out in the newspapers that her husband was very much surprised when he found that his wife had managed to get aboard in disguise. But Arago, one of the scientific staff, tells us in his Memoirs, published in 1837, that—as we can well believe—Freycinet knew perfectly who the "young and pretty" boy was, and had connived at her joining the ship as a lad, because she wanted to accompany her husband, and the authorities would have prevented her had they known. She continued to wear her boy's dress until after the ships visited Gibraltar, for Arago informs us that the solemn British Lieutenant-Governor there, when he saw her, broke into a smile, "the first perhaps that his features had worn for ten years." If that be true, the little lady surely did a little good by her saucy escapade. But official society regarded the lady in trousers with a frigid stare, so that henceforth she deemed it discreet to resume feminine garments. It does not appear that she passed for a boy when the expedition visited Sydney, and of course no hint of Madame's presence is given in the official history of the voyage.

We now reach the stage when the veil was lifted and the mystery explained. In 1813 the East India Company's ship HUNTER, voyaging from Calcutta to Sydney, called at the Fiji Islands. They discovered that several Europeans were living on one of the group. Some had been shipwrecked; some had deserted from vessels; but they had become accustomed to the life and preferred it. The HUNTER employed a party of them to collect sandal wood and beche-de-mer, one of her junior officers, Peter Dillon, being in charge. A quarrel with natives occurred, and all the Europeans were murdered, except Dillon, a Prussian named Martin Bushart, and a seaman, William Wilson. After the affray Bushart would certainly have been slain had he remained, so he induced the captain of the HUNTER to give him a passage to the first land reached. Accordingly Bushart, a Fiji woman who was his wife, and a Lascar companion, were landed on Barwell Island, or Tucopia.

Thirteen years later Peter Dillon was sailing in command of his own ship, the ST. PATRICK, from Valparaiso to Pondicherry, when he sighted Tucopia. Curiosity prompted him to stop to enquire whether his old friend Martin Bushart was still alive. He hove to, and shortly after two canoes put off from the land, bringing Bushart and the Lascar, both in excellent health.

Now, Dillon observed that the Lascar sold an old silver sword guard to one of the ST. PATRICK'S crew in return for a few fish hooks. This made him inquisitive. He asked the Prussian where it came from. Bushart informed him that when he first arrived at the island he saw in possession of the natives, not only this sword guard, but also several chain plates, iron bolts, axes, the handle of a silver fork, some knives, tea cups, beads, bottles, a silver spoon bearing a crest and monogram, and a sword. He asked where these articles were obtained, and the natives told him that they got them from the Mannicolo (or Vanikoro) cluster of islands, two days' canoe voyage from Tucopia, in the Santa Cruz group.

"Upon examining the sword minutely" wrote Dillon, "I discovered, or thought I discovered, the initials of Perouse stamped on it, which excited my suspicion and made me more exact in my inquiries. I then, by means of Bushart and the Lascar, questioned some of the islanders respecting the way in which their neighbours procured the silver and iron articles. They told me that the natives of Mannicolo stated that many years ago two large ships arrived at their islands; one anchored at the island of Whanoo, and the other at the island of Paiou, a little distance from each other. Some time after they anchored, and before they had any communication with the natives, a heavy gale arose and both vessels were driven ashore. The ship that was anchored off Whanoo grounded upon the rocks.

"The natives came in crowds to the seaside, armed with clubs, spears, and bows and arrows, and shot some arrows into the ship, and the crew in return fired the guns and some musketry on them and killed several. The vessel, continuing to beat violently against the rocks, shortly afterwards went to pieces. Some of the crew took to their boats, and were driven on shore, where they were to a man murdered on landing by the infuriated natives. Others threw themselves into the sea; but if they reached the shore it was only to share the fate of their wretched comrades, so that not a single soul escaped out of this vessel."

The ship wrecked on Paiou, according to the natives' story, was driven on a sandy beach. Some arrows were fired into her, but the crew did not fire. They were restrained, and held up beads, axes, and toys, making a demonstration of friendliness. As soon as the wind abated, an old chief came aboard the wrecked ship, where he was received in friendly fashion, and, going ashore, pacified his people. The crew of the vessel, compelled to abandon her, carried the greater part of their stores ashore, where they built a small boat from the remains of the wreck. As soon as this craft was ready to sail, as many as could conveniently be taken embarked and sailed away. They were never heard of again. The remainder of the crew remained on the island until they died.

Such was the information collected by Captain Peter Dillon in 1826. He took away with him the sword guard, but regretted to learn that the silver spoon had been beaten into wire by Bushart for making rings and ornaments for female islanders.

When he reached Calcutta, Dillon wrote an account of his discovery in a letter to the government of Bengal, and suggested that he should be sent in command of an expedition to search the Vanikoro cluster in the hope of finding some old survivor of Laperouse's unhappy company, or at all events further remains of the ships. He had prevailed upon Martin Bushart to accompany him to India, and hoped, through this man's knowledge of the native tongue, to elicit all that was to be known.

The Government of British India became interested in Dillon's discovery, and resolved to send him in command of a ship to search for further information. At the end of 1826 he sailed in the RESEARCH, and in September of the following year came within sight of the high-peaked island Tucopia. The enquiries made on this voyage fully confirmed and completed the story, and left no room for doubt that the ships of Laperouse had been wrecked and his whole company massacred or drowned on or near Vanikoro. Many natives still living remembered the arrival of the French. Some of them related that they thought those who came on the big ships to be not men but spirits; and such a grotesque bit of description as was given of the peaks of cocked hats exactly expressed the way in which the appearance of the strangers would be likely to appeal to the native imagination:—"There was a projection from their foreheads or noses a foot long."

Furthermore, Dillon's officers were able to purchase from the islands such relics as an old sword blade, a rusted razor, a silver sauce-boat with fleur-de-lis upon it, a brass mortar, a few small bells, a silver sword-handle bearing a cypher, apparently a "P" with a crown, part of a blacksmith's vice, the crown of a small anchor, and many other articles. An examination of natives brought out a few further details, as for example, a description of the chief of the strangers, "who used always to be looking at the stars and the sun and beckoning to them," which is how a native would be likely to regard a man making astronomical observations. Dillon, in short had solved the forty years' mystery. The Pacific had revealed her long-held secret.

It happened that a new French expedition in the ASTROLABE, under the command of Dumont-D'Urville, was in the southern hemisphere at this time. While he lay at Hobart on his way to New Zealand, the captain heard of Dillon's discoveries, and, at once changing his plans, sailed for the Santa Cruz Islands. He arrived there in February, 1828, and made some valuable finds to supplement those of the English captain. At the bottom of the sea, in perfectly clear water, he saw lying, encrusted with coral, some remains of anchors, chains, guns, bullets, and other objects which had clearly belonged to the ships of Laperouse. One of his artists made a drawing of them on the spot. They were recovered, and, together with Dillon's collection, are now exhibited in a pyramid at the Marine Museum at the Louvre in Paris, in memory of the ill-fated commander and crew who perished, martyrs in the great cause of discovery, a century and a quarter ago.

It is interesting to note that descendants of Captain Dillon are residents of Sydney to this day.

Chapter X.

THE FAME OF LAPEROUSE.

Intellectually, and as a navigator, Laperouse was a son of James Cook, and he himself would have rejoiced to be so described. The allusions to his predecessor in his writings are to be numbered by scores, and the note of reverent admiration is frequently sounded. He followed Cook's guidance in the management of his ships, paying particular attention to the diet of his crews. He did not succeed in keeping scurvy at bay altogether, but when the disease made its appearance he met it promptly by securing fresh vegetable food for the sufferers, and was so far successful that when he arrived in Botany Bay his whole company was in good health.

The influence of the example and experience of Cook may be illustrated in many ways, some of them curious. We may take a point as to which he really had little to fear; but he knew what had occurred in Cook's case and he was anxious that the same should not happen to him. The published story of Cook's first South Sea Voyage, as is well known, was not his own. His journal was handed over to Dr. Hawkesworth, a gentleman who tried to model his literary style on that of Dr. Johnson, and evolved a pompous, big-drum product in consequence. Hawkesworth garnished the manly, straightforward navigator's simple and direct English with embellishments of his own. Where Cook was plain Hawkesworth was ornate; where Cook was sensible Hawkesworth was silly; where Cook was accurate, Hawkesworth by stuffing in his own precious observations made the narrative unreliable, and even ridiculous. In fact, the gingerbread Johnson simply spoiled Cook.

Dr. Johnson was by no means gratified by the ponderous prancings of his imitator. We learn from Boswell that when the great man met Captain Cook at a dinner given by the President of the Royal Society, he said that he "was much pleased with the conscientious accuracy of that celebrated circumnavigator, who set me right as to many of the exaggerated accounts given by Dr. Hawkesworth of his voyages." Cook himself was annoyed by the decorating of his story, and resented the treatment strongly.

Laperouse knew this, and was very anxious that nobody in France should Hawkesworthify him. He did not object to being carefully edited, but he did not want to be decorated. He wrote excellent French narrative prose, and his work may be read with delight. Its qualities of clarity, picturesqueness and smoothness, are quite in accord with the fine traditions of the language. But, as it was likely that part of the history of his voyage might be published before his return, he did not want it to be handed over to anybody who would trick it out in finery, and he therefore wrote the following letter:

"If my journal be published before my return, let the editing of it by no means be entrusted to a man of letters; for either he will sacrifice to the turn of a phrase the proper terms which the seaman and man of learning would prefer, but which to him will appear harsh and barbarous; or, rejecting all the nautical and astronomical details, and endeavouring to make a pleasing romance, he will for want of the knowledge his education has not allowed him to acquire, commit mistakes which may prove fatal to those who shall follow me. But choose an editor versed in the mathematical sciences, who is capable of calculating and comparing my data with those of other investigators, of rectifying errors which may have escaped me, and of guarding himself against the commission of others. Such an editor will preserve the substance of the work; will omit nothing that is essential; will give technical details the harsh and rude, but concise style of a seaman; and will well perform his task in supplying my place and publishing the work as I would have done it myself."

That letter is a rather singular effect of Laperouse's study of Cook, which might be illustrated by further examples. The influence of the great English sailor is the more remarkable when we remember that there had been early French navigators to the South Seas before Laperouse. There was the elder Bougainville, the discoverer of the Navigator Islands; there was Marion-Dufresne, who was killed and eaten by Maoris in 1772; there was Surville—to mention only three. Laperouse knew of them, and mentioned them. But they had little to teach him. In short and in truth, he belonged to the school of Cook, and that is an excellent reason why English and especially Australian people should have an especial regard for him.

The disastrous end of Laperouse's expedition before he had completed his task prevented him from adequately realising his possibilities as a discoverer. As pointed out in the preceding pages, if he had completed his voyage, he would in all probability have found the southern coasts of Australia in 1788. But the work that he actually did is not without importance; and he unquestionably possessed the true spirit of the explorer. When he entered upon this phase of his career he was a thoroughly experienced seaman. He was widely read in voyaging literature, intellectually well endowed, alert-minded, eager, courageous, and vigorous. The French nation has had no greater sailor than Laperouse.

De Lesseps, the companion of his voyage as far as Kamchatka, has left a brief but striking characterisation of him. "He was," says this witness, "an accomplished gentleman, perfectly urbane and full of wit, and possessed of those charming manners which pertained to the eighteenth century. He was always agreeable in his relations with subordinates and officers alike." The same writer tells us that when Louis XVI gave him the command of the expedition he had the reputation of being the ablest seaman in the French navy.

Certainly he was no common man to whose memory stands that tall monument at Botany Bay. It was erected at the cost of the French Government by the Baron de Bougainville, in 1825, and serves not only as a reminder of a fine character and a full, rich and manly life, but of a series of historical events that are of capital consequence in the exploration and occupation of Australia.

It will be appropriate to conclude this brief biography with a tribute to the French navigator from the pen of an English poet. Thomas Campbell is best remembered by such vigorous poems as "Ye Mariners of England," and "The Battle of the Baltic," which express a tense and elevated British patriotism. All the more impressive for that very reason is his elegy in honour of a sailor of another nation, whose merits as a man and whose charm as a writer Campbell had recognised from his boyhood. The following are his.

LINES WRITTEN IN A BLANK LEAF OF LAPEROUSE'S "VOYAGES"

> Loved Voyager! whose pages had a zest
> More sweet than fiction to my wondering breast,

When, rapt in fancy, many a boyish day
I tracked his wanderings o'er the watery way,
Roamed round the Aleutian isles in waking dreams,
Or plucked the fleur-de-lys by Jesso's streams,
Or gladly leaped on that far Tartar strand,
Where Europe's anchor ne'er had bit the sand,
Where scarce a roving wild tribe crossed the plain,
Or human voice broke nature's silent reign, —
But vast and grassy deserts feed the bear,
And sweeping deer-herds dread no hunter's snare.
Such young delight his real records brought,
His truth so touched romantic springs of thought,
That, all my after life, his fate and fame
Entwined romance with Laperouse's name.
Fair were his ships, expert his gallant crews,
And glorious was the emprise of Laperouse —
Humanely glorious! Men will weep for him,
When many a guilty martial fame is dim:
He ploughed the deep to bind no captive's chain —
Pursued no rapine — strewed no wreck with slain;
And, save that in the deep themselves lie low,
His heroes plucked no wreath from human woe.
'Twas his the earth's remotest bounds to scan,
Conciliating with gifts barbaric man —
Enrich the world's contemporaneous mind,
And amplify the picture of mankind.
Far on the vast Pacific, 'midst those isles
O'er which the earliest morn of Asia smiles,
He sounded and gave charts to many a shore
And gulf of ocean new to nautic lore;
Yet he that led discovery o'er the wave,
Still finds himself an undiscovered grave.
He came not back! Conjecture's cheek grew pale,
Year after year; in no propitious gale
His lilied banner held its homeward way,
And Science saddened at her martyr's stay.
An age elapsed: no wreck told where or when
The chief went down with all his gallant men,
Or whether by the storm and wild sea flood

He perished, or by wilder men of blood.
The shuddering fancy only guess'd his doom,
And doubt to sorrow gave but deeper gloom.
An age elapsed: when men were dead or gray,
Whose hearts had mourned him in their youthful day,
Fame traced on Vanikoro's shore at last,
The boiling surge had mounted o'er his mast.
The islesmen told of some surviving men,
But Christian eyes beheld them ne'er again.
Sad bourne of all his toils—with all his band
To sleep, wrecked, shroudless, on a savage strand!
Yet what is all that fires a hero's scorn
Of death?—the hope to live in hearts unborn.
Life to the brave is not its fleeting breath,
But worth—foretasting fame that follows death.
That worth had Laperouse, that meed he won.
He sleeps—his life's long stormy watch is done.
In the great deep, whose boundaries and space
He measured, fate ordained his resting place;
But bade his fame, like th' ocean rolling o'er
His relics, visit every earthly shore.
Fair Science on that ocean's azure robe
Still writes his name in picturing the globe,
And paints (what fairer wreath could glory twine?)
His watery course—a world-encircling line.